The Lord Is My Shepherd

The Twenty-third Psalm

Illustrated by
Tom LaPadula

A GOLDEN BOOK · NEW YORK

Western Publishing Company, Inc., Racine, Wisconsin 53404

The psalms are beautiful prayers that people sing. People have offered psalms in prayer since Bible times.

A shepherd is a person who tends a flock of sheep. He guides the sheep, makes sure they have plenty to eat and drink, keeps them from harm, and watches over them at all times.

People believe that some of the psalms were written by King David, a shepherd who became the leader of all Israel.

The psalm in this book is about another King who is also a Shepherd—God, who tends His flock with patient loving-kindness every day.

The Lord is my Shepherd; I shall not want.

He maketh me to lie down in green pastures.

He leadeth me beside the still waters.

He restoreth my soul.

He leadeth me in the paths of righteousness, for His name's sake.

Yea, though I walk through the valley of the shadow of death, I will fear no evil, for Thou art with me.

Thy rod and Thy staff, they comfort me.

Thou preparest a table before me
in the sight of mine enemies.

Thou anointest my head with oil. My cup runneth over.

Surely goodness and mercy shall follow me all the days of my life, and I shall dwell in the house of the Lord forever.

The Twenty-third Psalm

Scottish Psalter, 1650

1. The Lord's my Shep-herd, I'll not want; He
2. My soul He doth re-store a-gain; And
3. Yea, though I walk in death's dark vale, Yet
4. My ta-ble Thou hast fur-nish-ed In
5. Good-ness and mer-cy all my life Shall

makes me down to lie In pas-tures green; He
me to walk doth make With-in the paths of
will I fear no ill; For Thou art with me,
pres-ence of my foes; My head Thou dost with
sure-ly fol-low me; And in God's house for-

Amen.